Fact Finders®

Ancient Egyptian Civilization

Ancient Egyptian
Hieroglyphs

by Kathy Allen

Consultant:
Jennifer Houser Wegner, PhD
Associate Curator, Egyptian Section
Penn Museum, Pennsylvania

CAPSTONE PRESS
a capstone imprint

Fact Finder Books are published by Capstone Press,
1710 Roe Crest Drive, North Mankato, Minnesota 56003
www.capstonepub.com

 Books published by Capstone Press are manufactured with paper
containing at least 10 percent post-consumer waste.

Library of Congress Cataloging-in-Publication Data
Allen, Kathy.
  Ancient Egyptian hieroglyphs / by Kathy Allen.
     p. cm. — (Fact finders. Ancient Egyptian civilization)
  Includes bibliographical references and index.
  Summary: "Describes the hieroglyphic writing system of ancient Egypt"—Provided by publisher.
  ISBN 978-1-4296-7627-4 (library binding)
  ISBN 978-1-4296-7976-3 (paperback)
  1. Egyptian language—Writing, Hieroglyphic—Juvenile literature. I. Title. II. Series.

  PJ1097.A44 2012
  493'.111—dc23   2011036737

Editorial Credits
Mari Bolte, editor; Juliette Peters, designer; Marcie Spence,
    photo researcher; Laura Manthe, production specialist

Photo Credits
Art Resource, N.Y.: Alfredo Dagli Orti, 12, Werner Forman, 16; Bridgeman Art Library: British
Museum, London, UK, 5, Egyptian National Museum, Cairo, Egypt, 14 (left), Look and Learn,
6, 25 (top), Louvre, Paris, France/Giraudon, 20, 25 (bottom), Royal Society, London, UK, 18;
Corbis: Gianni Dagli Orti, 15, Sandro Vannini, 23, Thomas Hartwell, 17; Dreamstime: Jorge Farres
Sanchez, 14 (right); Shutterstock: Bill McKelvie, 10, Dudarev Mikhail, design element, Efremova
Irina, 21, Fedor Selivanov, cover, 8, Rafa Irusta, design element, Tawfik Deifalla, 24 (left), Vladimir
Korostyshevskiy, 24 (right)

Printed in the United States of America in North Mankato, Minnesota.

042012   006696

TABLE OF CONTENTS

Mysterious Markings

In 1798 a group of French soldiers arrived in Egypt as part of an ongoing war with Britain. The soldiers were ordered to travel to Cairo on foot. It was a difficult trip during the hottest time of the year. The soldiers were not used to such hot sun and dry air. They were not prepared for a march through the desert. Many did not bring water. Dry biscuits were all they had to eat.

After many days in the sandy desert, the soldiers came upon an **oasis**. They saw a shimmering lake and palm trees. But as soon as they neared the water, it vanished. It was yet another **mirage**. When they began to see tombs and temples, they thought these, too, were tricks of the eye. When they touched the temples, they knew their visions were real. The structures were covered with some kind of picture writing. But nobody could read what it said.

oasis: a place in the desert where there is water

mirage: something that appears to be there but is not

When a soldier found a giant stone near the town of Rosetta, he barely trusted his tired eyes. At first he saw more of the strange markings no one could read. But the Rosetta stone was different from the others. He recognized Greek text carved into the stone. Could this text help them decode the writing on the walls and sculptures around them? What would they learn from this lost language?

FACTS

Scientists believe that the Rosetta stone is part of a larger piece. The rest of the stone has never been found.

the Rosetta stone

Chapter 1

Words of the Gods

The soldiers did not know that the strange lettering was part of an ancient language. The markings were a kind of writing called hieroglyphs. Hieroglyphic writing uses pictures to represent words. The word *hieroglyphs* means "God's words." Ancient Egyptians used these signs to tell tales of wars and gods. They carved them on tombs and temples. For more than 3,000 years, hieroglyphs were used to write their spoken language. But that skill was lost over time.

Scholars were brought to Egypt to study the stone.

It is easy to understand why hieroglyphs were difficult to read. They are much more than just rows of pictures. Hieroglyphs include signs that were pronounced and signs that weren't. Many signs can represent either an object or a sound. And some signs stand for both.

Signs that were pronounced are called phonograms. Some phonograms represented ideas. These signs are called ideograms. Each ideogram represented a word.

Ideograms

sound	symbol	meaning
r		"mouth"
pr		"house"
s		"man"
rc		"sun"

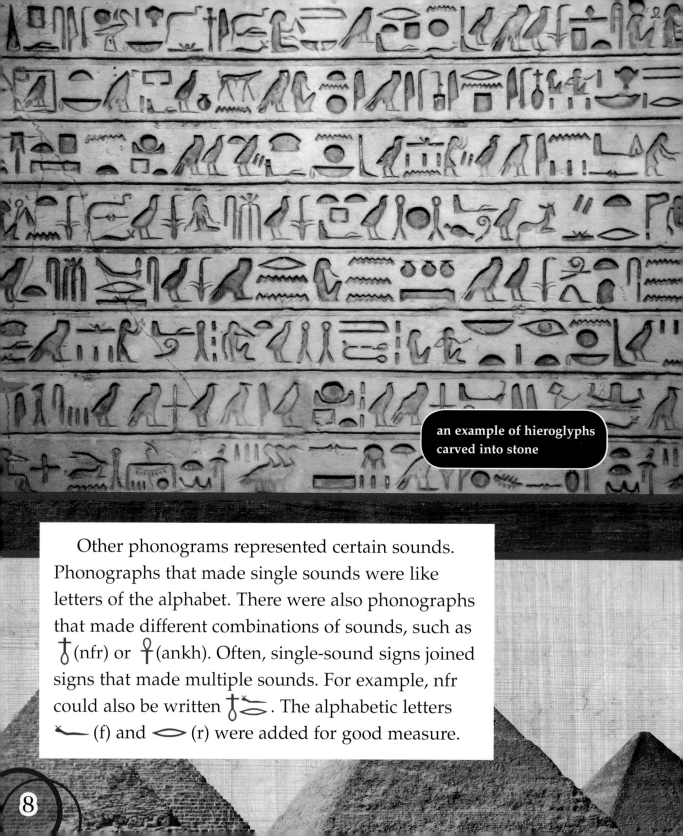

an example of hieroglyphs carved into stone

Other phonograms represented certain sounds. Phonographs that made single sounds were like letters of the alphabet. There were also phonographs that made different combinations of sounds, such as ⚚(nfr) or ☥(ankh). Often, single-sound signs joined signs that made multiple sounds. For example, nfr could also be written ⚚⌣. The alphabetic letters ⌣ (f) and ⌐ (r) were added for good measure.

Signs that were not pronounced were called determinatives. These signs came at the end of the written word. They made the meaning of the word more clear to the reader.

► Determinative ◄

sound	symbol	meaning
dgỉ		"look"
šp		"blind"
dpt		"ship"
ḫdỉ		"sail downstream"

Sometimes ideograms were used as determinatives. They were not pronounced.

sound	symbol	meaning
hrw		"day"
wbn		"rise"
smr		"courtier"
ꜥt		"room, chamber"
Ȝḫ		"horizon"
ỉwnn		"sanctuary"

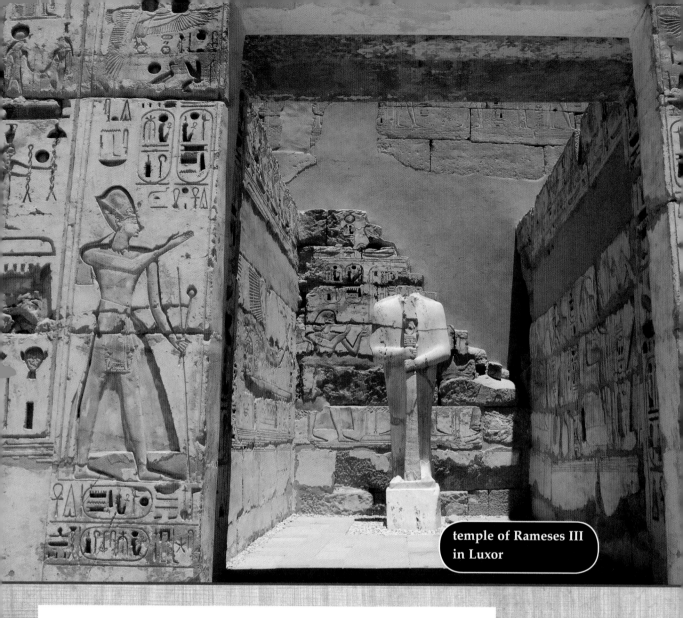

temple of Rameses III
in Luxor

Hieroglyphs are most often read from right to
left. But some monuments in Egypt have carvings
that are read from left to right. This difference is
because the hieroglyphs were also used to decorate
objects. The words meant the same thing. They may
have looked more balanced when written left to right.

It was important for the ancient Egyptians that those decorations be balanced on each side. A carving would often have two columns of hieroglyphs. One column was to be read from left to right. The other was to be read from right to left. The figures in the text showed how it should be read. For example, if the signs faced left, such as 𓅃 or 𓆇, they should be read from left to right.

Hieroglyphs are written in blocks. The ancient Egyptians loved things to be **symmetrical** and pleasing to the eye. For example, a string of signs would ideally be grouped in a blocklike formation. The signs ⌒⌒⊙𓀁 spell the name of the sun god, Ra. When grouped, they look like this: 𓂋𓁐. The taller pictures are balanced with wider pictures.

symmetry: a perfect balance along a center line

Something's Missing

You may notice that there is no punctuation or spacing between the hieroglyphs. There are also no vowels. Scholars still don't know today what vowels were used. This means that nobody knows exactly how to pronounce any one word in hieroglyphs.

Chapter 2

A Hieroglyphic History

a group of scribes

FACT

Less than 5 percent of the total population in ancient Egypt could write hieroglyphs.

The ancient Egyptians developed hieroglyphic writing around 3200 BC. Originally there were between 700 and 800 hieroglyphs, or glyphs for short. These glyphs were used to record prayers, spells, and religious texts. They were also used for recordkeeping.

By 300 BC, there were more than 6,000 signs. Only the most important people, such as the royal family, priests, and government workers, knew how to write hieroglyphs. Others who were trained to read and write hieroglyphs were called scribes. These scribes copied government and legal documents that were written in hieroglyphs. A scribe went through years of training to learn the signs and how to write them. Some went to scribal schools when they were as young as 12 years old.

Being a scribe was a good job. Scribes could earn a good living. But it was not easy work. A scribe could be seen studying or working for hours on end. There was a lot to learn. A student just starting to read and write hieroglyphs needed to know the meaning of at least 200 signs. A basic knowledge of hieroglyphs was around 750 signs. A fairly skilled scribe had to know more than 3,000 glyphs.

Scribes wrote on **papyrus**. Papyrus was made from plant strips that were pounded together in a layered pattern. Sheets of papyrus could be pressed together to make a long roll. Scribes wrote with a kind of brush made from reed plants. Cut reed stems were dipped in water. Then they were dipped in colors on a wooden block—like painting with watercolors. Black and red were used for general writing, while other colors were for illustration.

papyrus

a scribe kit

papyrus: a writing material made from plants

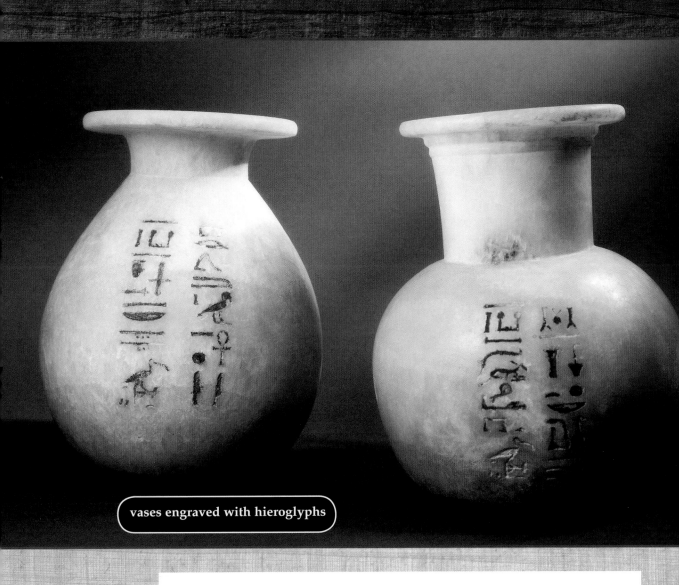

vases engraved with hieroglyphs

Craftsmen carved or painted hieroglyphs onto stone, pottery, wood, leather, and metal. The first signs found on pottery or small ivory plaques date back to 3200 BC. These earliest signs cannot be read easily. The first scribes worked with far fewer signs than later scribes. Eventually scribes used thousands of signs.

Along with hieroglyphs, the Egyptians also used a script called hieratic. This script was like cursive. The signs were more connected and could be written faster.

Hieratic script was not carved into stone but used for common documents such as letters. This kind of writing played an important role in the lives of everyday Egyptians.

hieroglyphs (left), and hieratic (right)

Along with being faster to write, hieratic was also always read the same way, from right to left. Special tools were used to make the script easier to write. The stems of rushes were cut to be more like a brush for this cursive writing.

Scribes began using another script called Demotic around 660 BC. Demotic was an abbreviated script. The signs looked nothing like hieroglyphs. The letters could be written even faster than hieratic. At first, Demotic was used only for official documents and letters. It was later used for all types of texts.

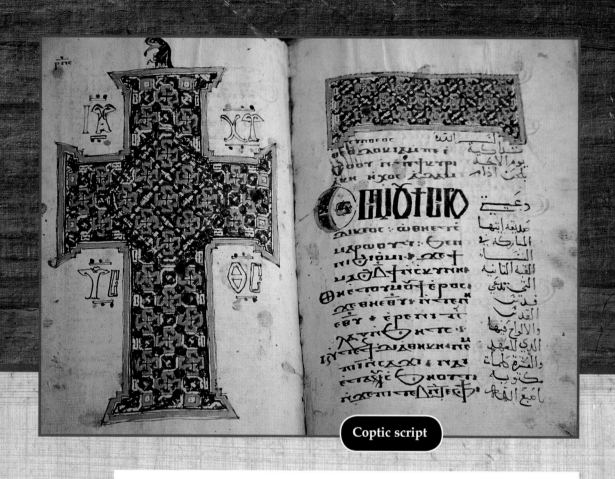

Coptic script

Coptic was the last script used to write the ancient Egyptian language. Developed around AD 200, Coptic uses Greek letters and a few Demotic signs. The name Coptic comes from the Greek word for Egyptian.

Hieroglyphs continued to be used through the Ptolemaic period (305 BC–30 BC). As the Romans began to rule Egypt, fewer and fewer people could read or write hieroglyphic signs. The last example of anyone writing in hieroglyphs is from AD 394. For the next 2,000 years, no one would be able to read or write the signs.

Chapter 3

Decoding Hieroglyphs

The Rosetta stone found by the soldiers in 1798 was covered in hieroglyphs, Demotic, and Greek writing. Copies of the writings were made and sent to scholars around the world. The Greek writing was decoded in 1802. The stone told of good deeds done by a ruler named Ptolemy V.

It would take more than 20 years to crack the rest of the code. The first scholars who looked at the stone made a mistake. They thought each sign stood for an object or an idea. The Greeks had thought the same. But none of them knew that many of the signs stood for sounds too.

Thomas Young

An English doctor was the first scholar to see that the signs stood for sounds. In 1814 Thomas Young received a copy of the stone's writing. He noticed that a sign called a **cartouche** was used to circle the names of kings and queens. He wondered if he could find the names of Greek rulers circled in cartouches. He noticed that the Greek name Ptolemy looked very similar in both Greek and Demotic. He read through the hieroglyphs and found the same result with the Demotic writing and the hieroglyphs.

cartouche: an oval with a ruler's name inside it

Ptolemy

The ruler's name is spelled both Ptolemy and Ptolemaios. However, his name is pronounced the same no matter the spoken language. Young used this knowledge to match the glyphs to sounds. Young soon had a short vocabulary list of 86 words translated from Greek to Demotic.

The name Ptolemy written in both hieroglyphs (top) and Demotic (bottom)

Thomas Young's decipherment of the name Ptolemy from the Rosetta Stone text.

heiroglyph	Young's sound value	actual sound value
■	**p**	**P**
◠	**t**	**t**
⌀	optional	**o**
🦁	**lo** or **ole**	**l**
▭	**ma** or **m**	**m**
𝌆	**i**	**i** or **y**
⌐	**osh** or **os**	**s**

Jean-François
Champollion

Frenchman Jean-François Champollion followed Young's work closely. He took Young's vocabulary list and expanded it. After two years of work, Champollion was able to recognize the names and titles of most of the leaders mentioned in the text. He was also able to understand and explain the grammar system that was used.

At the time, many researchers believed that each hieroglyph stood for a sound. Names of rulers were written **phonetically**, just like Ptolemy's. Names such as Alexander or Cleopatra were written this way too. But in 1822, Champollion saw a cartouche that had an older, more traditional Egyptian name.

the cartouche
Champollion
studied in 1822

phonetics: a system of writing in which symbols directly represent sounds

Champollion did not know what the first two symbols meant. But he did know that the double symbol at the end made an "s" sound. He also knew the Coptic word for sun was "ra." He wondered if the Egyptian glyph meant the same thing. He thought the middle symbol, with its three prongs, might be an "m." Champollion also knew there had been a pharaoh named Rameses.

Names in cartouches written alongside regular hieroglyphs

FACT

Cartouches symbolized a loop made from a double thickness of rope. The ends of the rope were tied together. Cartouches were seen as symbols of eternity. Drawing a cartouche around someone's name made the sign into an amulet and protected that person.

To test his idea, Champollion searched for another cartouche with the same symbols. He used this cartouche as a comparison.

He knew the bird represented the god Thoth and used that as a starting point. By sounding the symbols out, he came up with the name of another pharaoh, Thutmose. By filling in the blanks, Champollion was able to prove that the hieroglyphs stood for both sounds and ideas.

Soon after, Champollion was finally able to read the entire Rosetta stone. He made a list of signs along with their meanings in Greek. After his death in 1832, his works were published as a dictionary and a grammar book.

FACT

The Rosetta stone was dated the same day it was carved—196 BC, the ninth year of Ptolemy V's rule.

The Book of the Dead

Another famous text written in hieroglyphs is called the *Book of the Dead*. The *Book of the Dead* originated in the New Kingdom (1539–1292 BC). This book was a collection of spells written on scrolls. It was also a place for scribes to record spells that would help the dead in the **afterlife**. The book was buried with the dead.

a page from the *Book of the Dead*

afterlife: the place where Egyptians believed a person's soul went after death

Hieroglyphs Through Time

Rule of
Tutankhamun

Alexander the Great enters
Egypt, putting the country
under Greek rule; the
Greco-Roman Period begins.

Humans settle
in Egypt.

Demotic is
developed.

Scribes use
several thousand
hieroglyphic signs.

| prior to 5000 BC | 1332–1323 BC | 660 BC | 332 BC | 300 BC |
| 3200 BC | 1187–1156 BC | 305 BC | | 196 BC |

The first use
of hieroglyphs
is recorded.

Ptolemaic dynasty
(Dynasty 33) begins

Rule of Rameses III

Rosetta stone
is carved.

The Greek writing on the Rosetta stone is translated.

Englishman Thomas Young translates the Demotic text of the Rosetta stone.

Cleopatra dies, beginning Roman rule in Egypt

The last use of hieroglyphs is recorded.

| 30 BC | August 24, 394 | 1802 | 1814 |

| 69 BC | AD 200 | August 1798 | 1822 |

Cleopatra VII is born.

The Rosetta stone is discovered.

Coptic is developed.

Frenchman Jean-François Champollion is able to read the entire Rosetta stone.

Chapter 4

Words and Numbers

The hieroglyphic alphabet had 24 signs for sounds. Again, there were no signs for some vowels in English such as "u" or "o." There was also no sign for the letter "v."

ah father	p pop	h ha	k kettle
i bill	f feet	kh lock	g good
ee easy	m mom	k lick	t toe
a car	n no	s see	ch church
oo too or w well	r roll	sh ship	d day
b boy	h hand	q Iraq	j jazz

Numbers in hieroglyphs were based on signs that stood for units of 10. The sign I was used to write numbers between one and nine. For example, III was three and IIII was four.

Larger numbers used more than one kind of sign added together. Tens, hundreds, thousands, and other multiples of 10 had their own symbols. For example, the number 276 looked like this:

276

Chapter 5

Write Your Own

Use the alphabet on page 26 to write your name in hieroglyphs. Remember that hieroglyphs were written without vowels. So, Jenny would become J N N Y. Using the letter chart, those sounds in hieroglyphs are [hieroglyphs]. Hieroglyphs should be balanced, so this string could become [hieroglyphs]. Your name may have a letter not in the alphabet on page 26. If so, it's your lucky day and you get to make your own sign! And if you're feeling royal, why not add a cartouche?

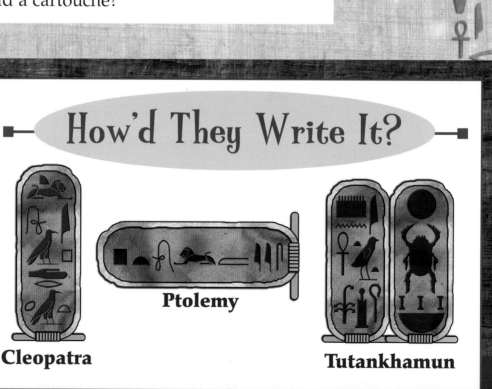

How'd They Write It?

Ptolemy

Cleopatra

Tutankhamun

What's His Name?

Pharaohs had five different names. Three names represented the gods—the Horus, Nebti, and Golden Horus name. They also had a throne name and birth or family name. The pharaohs are generally known by their throne name, also called the prenomen, and their birth name, also called the nomen.

The prenomen and nomen are written in cartouches. The other names are not. King Tut's names appear on the left page. The cartouche on the left is his birth name, Tutankhamun. The cartouche on the right is his throne name, Nebkheperure.

FACT

Names were important to ancient Egyptians. They believed that if a person's name was not written anywhere, the person could not survive in the afterlife. They wrote their names in their tombs and graves in the hopes that the writing would last forever.

Today historians use hieroglyphs to learn more about ancient Egypt. Just glancing at some glyphs on a jar can tell them a lot. They can learn who owned the jar, where and when the person lived, and what their beliefs were. They can learn about a ruler's rise to power and a god's special ability. Hieroglyphs tell a story, and the discovery of the Rosetta stone made retelling the story possible.

GLOSSARY

afterlife (AF-tur-life)—the place where Egyptians believed a person's soul went after death

amulet (AM-yoo-let)—a small charm believed to protect the wearer from harm

cartouche (kar-TOOSH)—an oval with a ruler's name inside it; a nameplate or name tag

mirage (muh-RAZH)—something that appears to be there but is not; mirages are caused by light rays bending where air layers of different temperatures meet

oasis (oh-AY-siss)—a place in the desert where there is water; plants and trees grow in oases

papyrus (puh-PYE-ruhss)—a tall water plant that grows in northern Africa and southern Europe; a material that is written on can be made from the stems of this plant

phonetics (FUH-net-iks)—a system of writing in which symbols directly represent sounds

symmetry (SIM-uh-tree)—a perfect balance along a center line

READ MORE

Corrick, James A. *Gritty, Stinky Ancient Egypt: The Disgusting Details about Life in Ancient Egypt.* Disgusting History. Mankato, Minn.: Capstone Press, 2011.

Deady, Kathleen W. *Ancient Egypt: Beyond the Pyramids.* Great Civilizations. Mankato, Minn.: Capstone Press, 2012.

Kennett, David. *Pharaoh: Life and Afterlife of a God.* New York: Walker & Company, 2008.

INTERNET SITES

FactHound offers a safe, fun way to find Internet sites related to this book. All of the sites on FactHound have been researched by our staff.

Here's all you do:

Visit *www.facthound.com*

Type in this code: 9781429676274

Super-cool stuff!

Check out projects, games and lots more at
www.capstonekids.com

INDEX